As is natural, some "pot-shots" miss their mark. Some are—again, natural enough—merely platitudes stood on their heads so as to give the appearance of paradoxes. But others are witty, unexpected, charming, wry—most enjoyable.

—*Clifton Fadiman*

I MAY NOT BE TOTALLY PERFECT, BUT PARTS OF ME ARE EXCELLENT

© 1973)

And Other
BRILLIANT THOUGHTS ®

By
ASHLEIGH BRILLIANT

Woodbridge Press Publishing Company
Santa Barbara, California 93111

1994 Printing

Published by

Woodbridge Press Publishing Company
Post Office Box 209
Santa Barbara, California 93102

Distributed simultaneously in the United States and Canada.

Printed in the United States of America.

Library of Congress Cataloging-in-Publication Data

Brilliant, Ashleigh, 1933-

   I may not be totally perfect, but parts of me are excellent, and other brilliant thoughts.

   1. Epigrams.   2. American wit and humor, pictorial.   I. Title
PN6281.B68   818'.5'402   79-10052
ISBN 0-912800-66-6   CIP
ISBN 0-912800-67-4 (pbk.)

Dedication

*Part of this Book
is Dedicated to You,
and the Rest
to You-Know-Who.*

Ashleigh
Brilliant

TRY TO BE
THE BEST OF
WHATEVER YOU ARE,

EVEN IF
WHAT YOU ARE
IS
NO GOOD.

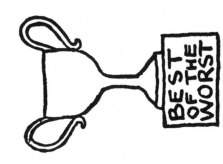

In This Book . . .

How Do I Do? 9

Communication 17

People Are Like That 27

You and Me 43

The Strange World of Other People 61

Time and Change 75

The World and Other Illusions 85

What Is Your Pleasure? 97

A Thousand Thinks 105

Life and Other Problems 119

Health, Death and Other
    Mysterious Conditions 137

The Crowded Self 147

I MAY NOT BE
TOTALLY PERFECT,
BUT PARTS OF ME
ARE EXCELLENT.

Ashleigh
Brilliant

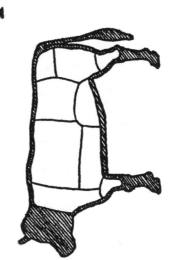

How Do I Do?

Ashleigh Brilliant is my real name. I was born (in England) in the same year that Franklin Roosevelt and Adolf Hitler began to rule the World (1933), and have never quite recovered from the shock of losing both of them when I was only eleven years old (1945).

The following purely malicious rumors about me are all true:

1. I was once arrested in Madrid for wearing shorts (1952).

2. I gave a public speech in Red Square, Moscow, on the subject of Human Rights, and was subsequently expelled from Russia (1959).

3. I was the first person ever to use the official University of California Free Speech Platform at Berkeley (April 12, 1962).

4. On April 7, 1967, I was publicly designated a "hippie" by the San Francisco *Examiner*.

5. In May, 1969, I was arrested in Cape Town, South Africa, for riding in a car with the sign, "ATTENTION CAR THIEVES—THIS CAR IS ALREADY STOLEN."

6. I was the subject of a major Free Speech demonstration at the University of Oregon (Eugene, February 3, 1965) at which twelve members of the faculty stood on the steps of the English department building, and gave a public reading of an "obscene" poem.

7. It took me fifteen years, instead of the usual five, to become a U.S. citizen, (August 26, 1969), because I was accused of having an immoral relationship with a woman whom I had produced as a witness to my good character.

8. The British headmaster who had once caned me at school for criticizing the teaching methods of one of my teachers, later applied to become my business agent (1971).

9. I am guilty of holding degrees from three Universities, and became a Doctor of Philosophy by writing an incredibly scholarly work on the *Social Effects of the Automobile in Southern California During the Nineteen-Twenties* (Berkeley, 1964).

10. I am also the author of the notorious *Haight-Ashbury Songbook* ("Songs of Love and Haight"), which Herb Caen of the San Francisco *Chronicle* denounced as "good clean fun," and which was (no doubt) a major corrupting influence in the celebrated San Francisco "Summer of Love" (1967).

11. My career as a professional teacher of history has been more or less awash ever since I taught for two round-the-world semester voyages on the famous "Floating University," then administered by Chapman College (1965-67).

12. My art work was considered so unacceptable for display in the Arts and Crafts Show of Santa Barbara, California, that a special law was passed to keep it out (1976).

13. As a candidate for the Santa Barbara City Council (1977), I conducted my entire campaign in song (and lost).

14. Patty Hearst once wrote to me and said, "You must be out of your mind, but I love it!!!"

So now you know something about me. Obviously, I am some kind of professional trouble-maker, working both inside and outside the system. Or, if you want to be more kind, you can call me a pioneer. This book is the result of a particular kind of pioneering effort which I have been making, with increasing seriousness, for most of my life—an attempt to say some important things (ideas which, of course, have all been expressed in some fashion before) in a new and perhaps better way. As you can see from my name, it requires no immodesty for me to call them *Brilliant Thoughts*. They have already been published under various other names, such as *Pot Shots*, and in a variety of media, but this is their first appearance under this name, and in book form.

How I Invented This Game

I would like to be able to say that from the very beginning I knew exactly what I was doing and had a careful plan, of which you see here the final and perfect result. The truth, of course, is nothing of the sort. It all began with miscellaneous bits of thinking which I jotted down from time to time on miscellaneous bits of paper, and, not knowing what else to do with them, I simply stashed them away.

When at last I couldn't stand keeping them to myself any longer, I began reading them aloud to groups of friends, calling them one-line poems, or "Unpoemed Titles." To emphasize that each line was a completely separate piece, I would pause between lines to make some kind of sounds on whatever sound-making instrument happened to be handy, and would encourage my audience to do the same.

Many people urged me to illustrate and publish these works, but I hesitated, seeking a form which would continue to put space between them. At last I hit on the idea of publishing them as *postcards*, which solved the problem nicely, and had several additional advantages. (1) The postcard form combined openness with intimacy, just as my writings were attempting to do. (2) It had a practical purpose: unlike an ordinary book, my "one-page books" could not only be *read*, but also *used*. (3) It was easy to become one's own publisher; and, assuming that the messages had commercial appeal (which, much to my surprise, soon became evident), the whole thing had tremendous business potential. My first cards were published in San Francisco in 1967, and, if you count each card as a separate work, I am surely by now one of the world's all-time best-selling authors.

At some early point in this undertaking, it occurred to me that I was in the process of creating something so new and different that it hardly fitted into any established category. In one sense, it was an entirely new form of literature. Of course, there have always been proverbs, epigrams, and "grafitti" of various kinds. But very few writers in our language (apart from the pitiable hacks of the greeting card industry) have ever devoted themselves to creating an extended series of such works; far fewer have ever asked or expected to be taken seriously as writers; and none, so far as I know, has ever attempted to publish each brief utterance as a separate copyrighted literary work. With all deference to Chairman Mao and other authors whose quotations derive from longer works, it seemed that I was becoming the world's first writer of self-contained ready-made quotations.

In another sense, the significance of my work seemed to be at least as much scientific and sociological as literary. I was creating a new kind of instantaneous communication. The entire message was right there, on one side of one piece of paper, and could be read in a flash. My postcards were what Marshall McLuhan might one day call the last gasp of Gutenburg—a bridge between the dying technology of print and the new age of electronic communication.

11

Convinced of the importance of what I was doing, I began to develop a set of rules and guidelines to give it distinct shape and character. The most important of these was *brevity*. No *Brilliant Thought* must ever exceed a maximum of seventeen words. Why seventeen? First, because, at the time I made the decision, I found that the longest line I had yet published had seventeen words. Secondly, I was perhaps influenced by knowing that the Japanese *Haiku* form of poetry is limited to exactly seventeen syllables (not words).

A second major rule was *universality*. One object of the game, I decided, was to reach as many minds, over as much of the world, and as far into the future, as possible. Therefore the words must be simple, easily understood, and easily translated. Their effect must not in any way depend upon rhyme, rhythm, puns, or any other kind of conventional word-play. For the same reason, all topical, local, and even cultural allusions must be avoided. On the other hand, in order to reach everybody, I must be free to discuss every conceivable topic, including those not necessarily considered very pleasant and those not commonly publicly aired at all. In particular, I wanted to say the kinds of things which most of us feel, but many of us find very difficult to express.

With so limited a format, the challenge was to pack the most possible insight, amusement, intelligence, and feeling into the fewest possible words. And, since "word-play" was ruled out, there must be free rein for "meaning-play," in such forms as irony, ambiguity, subtlety, audacity, paradox, and crazy logic.

The casual reader of these works is not usually aware of the high degree of discipline upon which they are based; but that, of course, is as it should be, and is itself the result of another of my rules: a *Brilliant Thought* should be expressed in something approximating ordinary colloquial speech. It should sound like something that somebody might say. But there is also the vital rule of *originality*, which demands that, to the best of my knowledge, it is substantially different from anything anybody ever actually *has* said before.

But what about the pictures? You will already have gathered that it is the words with which I am primarily concerned. And one of the intentional features of this work is that the words are not dependent on the "art" for their impact, and can be fully appreciated without any graphic accompaniment. This makes it very different from the conventional "panel cartoon," which usually consists of an illustration and a caption, which are both necessary for a full understanding and enjoyment of the work. In illustrating the words, I try to avoid depicting specific situations. I provide instead a sort of oblique commentary, leaving it to you, the reader, to find your own particular applications for the words. For the same reason, I have avoided the temptation to create a comic-strip-like "cast of characters," although you will find a bearded figure appearing occasionally, who remotely resembles me.

Am I Playing This Game, Or Is The Game Playing Me?

So, what happens when you spend years of your life putting pieces of your mind on thousands of cards, and sending them out to make their own way in the world? It was such a new game that I had no idea what to expect. I hoped vaguely to discover if there was anybody like me out there. I also wanted to see how far a person like me could go in a world like this, simply by being myself, and letting everybody know it.

The results have in many ways been very strange. For one thing, I soon discovered that *Everybody* out there is somehow like me, or at least they all seem to think they are, although often their only evidence is just one *Brilliant Thought* which they may have seen on a card or in a newspaper somewhere. People often write to me saying things like "I never knew anybody else had these thoughts and feelings. Now I don't feel so alone any more."

Another thing that happens is that, if people like what you are doing and think it will sell, they start coming to you with commercial schemes for doing many things with your work which you had never thought of doing. *You,* perhaps, had been hoping for recognition from scholars and critics. But *they* want to recognize it by printing it on paper cups and underpants. You pause (briefly) before signing the lucrative contract, knowing that no Pulitzer Prize has yet been awarded for paper cups or underpants. But then, you reflect, the times may change. . .

(Still, I must confess a certain pride in being possibly the only serious author privileged to see his own peculiar thoughts appearing on a wide variety of licensed products from tote-bags to cocktail-napkins, and even being publicly paraded around in the form of T-shirts on other people's chests. In one of my fantasies, I go about with a notebook, studying the chests of attractive persons who are wearing Ashleigh Brilliant T-Shirts, and, when asked what I'm doing, I reply: "I'm just collecting my thoughts.")

I'LL LISTEN TO YOUR UNREASONABLE DEMANDS

IF YOU'LL CONSIDER MY UNACCEPTABLE OFFER.

14

Something else, however, somewhat less pleasant, also happens if what you are doing appears to be at all successful: other people start copying it, and you have to decide what to do about this. Of course, you could decide to ignore it, and altruistically donate your priceless creations to the public domain. But I decided from the beginning that that was not my game. In the game I was playing, each of my creations was my property, and I was entitled to be protected from theft. So I carefully copyrighted all my works, and, whenever a case of infringement came up, I immediately took whatever legal action was necessary to stop it, regardless of cost. These actions are always successful in the end, but some of the cases have been so unusual that they are making legal history. In one case, one of my *Thoughts* (it happens also to be the title of this book) appeared without my authorization on a T-shirt worn in a network television "Movie of the Week." The makers of the film (Universal City Studios) eventually acknowledged my copyright and paid for the right to use my twelve words (at a very high rate per word). In another, much more complicated, case, which involved hiring lawyers in three different countries, a large firm in Germany was forced to stop translating my cards into Dutch and selling them in Holland. Even mighty *Time* magazine, after hearing from my lawyer concerning one of my *Thoughts* which they had reproduced without my permission and without credit (*Time*, July 27, 1970, p.8), agreed to publish an acknowledgement of my authorship and copyright (Sept. 14, 1970, p. 8). These have all been milestones in the long process of securing legitimacy at the highest levels for my hitherto unheard-of species of literary art.

But what about Fame? Is not that, too, part of the game? Like many others before me, I have been afflicted with a vision of greatness and a desire to enjoy whatever good things this world may have to offer, combined with a feeling that all is vanity. If one must be a celebrity, however, it is consoling to be celebrated for something so relatively harmless as creating a new medium of communication. And I never tire totally of being told that something I have said has been found cheering, meaningful, and useful to somebody else. People who know my work do tend to behave towards me in a respectful and even admiring manner which somehow seems strangely inconsistent with the nature of the work itself, and makes me feel somewhat like the perpetrator of a successful hoax. But when I look about me at my fellow celebrities (most of whom have come to public attention through existing media, rather than by creating their own), I often feel that, by comparison, my own contribution to the general welfare has been a substantial one.

You Too Can Play

One other fascinating result of this large-scale experiment in what is now called "consciousness-raising" has been the development of what may very well be one of the world's oddest mail-order businesses. Every single one of my messages is kept permanently in print on postcards which can be ordered by mail from my own company. This enables anybody anywhere in the world to choose at leisure from a vast range of messages, finding just the right ones for their own particular needs; and it enables me to have a direct type of contact with my public which few other writers enjoy.

If you would like to play this part of the game, please send for my catalogue, which lists all the cards, including many hundreds not in this book, and help spread the happy habit of using them for personal, business, and official purposes. The price of the catalogue, which comes with sample cards and a beautiful order form, is currently (1985) two U.S.dollars. Please enclose that amount, or its equivalent in your own time and currency. My address is:

Ashleigh Brilliant
117 W. Valerio Street,
Santa Barbara, California 93101, U.S.A.

Communication

Even in the long unhappy years before there were *Brilliant Thoughts,* postcards (which have been in existence since the 1860's) attempted with both printed words and (more especially) with printed pictures, to help people communicate with each other. The subject of communication itself, however, was rarely dealt with. As you will see in this section, I have attempted to remedy this deficiency.

But isn't there something ominous about the growing use of pre-fabricated messages? My post cards provide the senders with plenty of space to add their own personal messages—but what sort of things are they saying? It happens that Fate and the Post Office have provided me with an excellent way of finding out. Any undeliverable first-class mail is always returned by the Post Office to the sender. But frequently people who send one of my cards neglect to put a return address on it. If it proves undeliverable for any reason, then it gets returned to *me,* since my own name and address happen to be printed on it. Thus I now have quite a large collection of these "used" *Brilliant Thoughts.* One thing they reveal is that many of my messages apparently do the job so well that often the only comment added by the sender is something like "How true" or "Need I say more?"

So I'm helping people to communicate, but am I not also helping them to become more and more inarticulate? Sometimes I play with the idea that all human thoughts and feelings could be computerized, and, given any particular situation, the machine could in a flash present you with exactly the right thing to say. This of course immediately conjures up the image of another computer ready to receive the message and instantaneously produce the correct reply.

On the more positive side, however, I do feel that the idea of making available very small pieces of thought, feelings (and why not many other types of information?) in a handy convenient format which (unlike a book) is very easily carried on the person, posted on a wall, or sent in the mail, may actually be an extremely useful and effective way of humanizing the computeristic trend towards an ultimate total codification of the human mind. Perhaps not only our machines but we ourselves could make somewhat more sense of the universe if it were broken up into little uniform pieces for us all to play with.

COMMUNICATE!

IT CAN'T
MAKE THINGS
ANY WORSE.

I DON'T WISH TO APPEAR
OVERLY INQUISITIVE,
BUT ARE YOU STILL ALIVE?

POT-SHOTS NO. 281.

AGREE WITH ME NOW:

IT WILL SAVE SO MUCH TIME.

POT-SHOTS NO. 1078.

YES, BUT EVERY TIME I TRY TO SEE THINGS YOUR WAY,

I GET A HEADACHE.

Ashleigh Brilliant

POT-SHOTS NO. 734.

WHAT GOOD IS IT IF I TALK IN FLOWERS

WHILE YOU'RE THINKING IN PASTRY?

Ashleigh Brilliant

21

When all other means of communication fail,

try words.

Ashleigh Brilliant

I WAITED AND WAITED,

AND WHEN NO MESSAGE CAME,

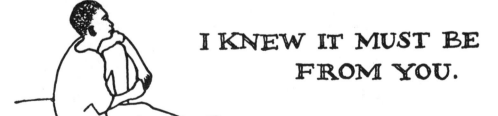

I KNEW IT MUST BE
FROM YOU.

Ashleigh Brilliant

22

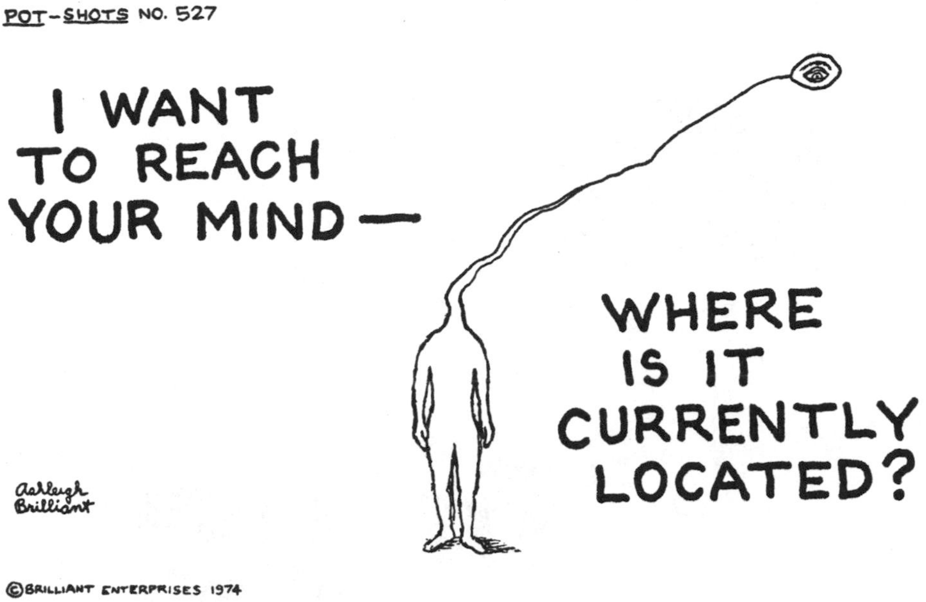

I WANT
TO REACH
YOUR MIND —

WHERE
IS IT
CURRENTLY
LOCATED?

*Ashleigh
Brilliant*

Ashleigh Brilliant

WHEN I
SAY NOTHING,
I DON'T
NECESSARILY
MEAN
NOTHING.

PEOPLE
RESPOND
TO PEOPLE
WHO RESPOND.

I DON'T
WANT TO
BORE YOU...

But there's nobody else around
for me to bore.

LET'S NOT COMPLICATE OUR RELATIONSHIP

BY TRYING TO COMMUNICATE WITH EACH OTHER.

Ashleigh Brilliant

WORDS CAN NEVER EXPRESS

WHAT WORDS CAN NEVER EXPRESS.

I'M WRITING
TO TELL YOU
I HAVE NOTHING TO SAY

Ashleigh Brilliant

Ashleigh Brilliant

INFORM ALL
THE TROOPS THAT
COMMUNICATIONS
HAVE
COMPLETELY
BROKEN
DOWN.

I'LL PRETEND TO
TRUST YOU . . . .

IF YOU'LL
PRETEND TO
TRUST ME.

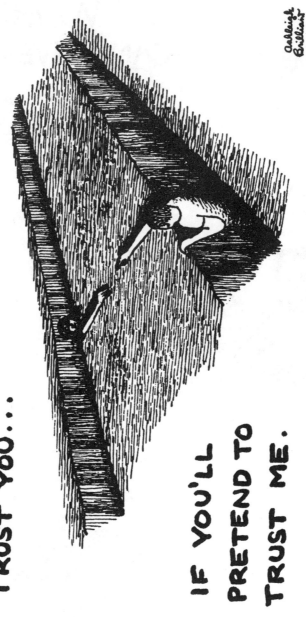

Ashleigh
Brilliant

People Are Like That

Human nature, like everything else, is changing. (In many ways, for example, we are much more kind, or at least less cruel, to people and creatures for whose feelings our ancestors had little regard). But here are some snapshots of it taken from a concealed position in the back of my own mind. I claim no special knowledge, other than perhaps an ability to savor the ridiculous. A drama critic might call my medium "The Postcard of the Absurd."

If you feel personally involved in many (or any) of these "snapshots," it is because I am like a good writer of horoscopes, whose art or contrivance it is to combine generalities and specifics in such a way that the reader can always find something to relate to. This (if you like) is a cheap trick, and it becomes cheaper (and more effective) the more I play it. The more different messages I put into circulation, the more chance there is that everybody will eventually be reached by, and pleased by, at least one.

But I don't want merely to amuse. Like every starry-eyed prophet, I want to help human nature keep changing and improving. And this series of little tricks is, I hope, one of the safer ways of doing it.

PLEASE DON'T PUT A STRAIN ON OUR FRIENDSHIP

BY
ASKING ME
TO DO SOMETHING
FOR YOU.

Ashleigh Brilliant

ACCEPT ME FOR WHAT I AM —

COMPLETELY
UNACCEPTABLE.

Ashleigh Brilliant

I HAVE JUST
DISCOVERED THE TRUTH,
AND CAN'T UNDERSTAND
WHY EVERYBODY
ISN'T EAGER
TO HEAR IT.

Ashleigh Brilliant

PLEASE
REMAIN
CALM

Ashleigh Brilliant

IT'S
NO USE
BOTH OF US
BEING
HYSTERICAL
AT THE
SAME TIME.

To any
truly impartial person,
it would be
obvious that
I am always right.

Ashleigh Brilliant

29

YOU ARE DEFINITELY ON MY LIST

BUT I'VE FORGOTTEN WHAT IT'S A LIST OF.

Ashleigh Brilliant

All I ask
of Life
is a constant
and exaggerated
sense of
my own importance.

The help I need
most urgently

is help in admitting

that I need help.

I NEED
SOME OF MY PROBLEMS

TO HELP
TAKE MY MIND OFF
SOME OF THE OTHERS.

Ashleigh Brilliant

MY BEST CONSOLATION
IS THE HOPE

THAT THE THINGS
I FAILED TO GET

WERE'NT REALLY
WORTH HAVING.

Ashleigh Brilliant

Ashleigh Brilliant

IF ONLY
I COULD GET
THAT WONDERFUL FEELING
OF ACCOMPLISHMENT

WITHOUT
HAVING TO
ACCOMPLISH
ANYTHING.

I CAN DO WITHOUT
THE ESSENTIALS,
BUT I MUST HAVE
MY LUXURIES.

Ashleigh Brilliant

POT-SHOTS NO. 576
Ashleigh
Brilliant

SAY SOMETHING YOU'LL BE SORRY FOR—

I love
receiving
apologies.

POT-SHOTS NO. 963.

THANK YOU FOR LETTING ME CRITICIZE YOU SO UNFAIRLY:

Ashleigh
Brilliant

IT MAKES ME
FEEL
SO
IMPORTANT.

POT-SHOTS NO. 449

MY MIND IS OPEN

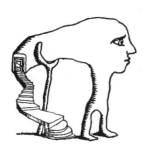

BY
APPOINTMENT
ONLY

THE TIME FOR ACTION IS PAST!

NOW IS THE TIME FOR SENSELESS BICKERING!

Ashleigh Brilliant

PLEASE FORGIVE ME IF, IN THE HEAT OF BATTLE,

I SOMETIMES FORGET WHICH SIDE I'M ON.

Ashleigh Brilliant

SOME OF THE THINGS
THAT WILL LIVE LONGEST
IN MY MEMORY

NEVER
REALLY
HAPPENED.

Ashleigh
Brilliant

I DEFINITELY INTEND
TO START LIVING
SOMETIME SOON.

I resent
being treated

like the sort of person
I really
am.

I DESPERATELY
NEED SOME
WISE
ADVICE

WHICH WILL
RECOMMEND
THAT I DO
WHAT I
WANT TO DO.

37

IT'S TIME FOR US
TO MAKE SOME BIG CHANGES —

WHY DON'T YOU CHANGE FIRST?

Ashleigh Brilliant

Ashleigh Brilliant

I CAN ADMIT TO MYSELF THAT I WAS WRONG,

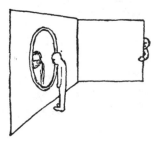

BUT I'LL NEVER ADMIT IT TO YOU.

EVERYBODY IS ENTITLED TO MY OPINION.

Ashleigh
Brilliant

BEEN THROUGH HELL?

AND WHAT DID YOU BRING BACK FOR ME?

YOU ARE ALWAYS
WELCOME
IN MY
TERRITORY

AT YOUR OWN RISK.

SEEING IS BELIEVING —

I WOULDN'T
HAVE SEEN IT
IF I HADN'T
BELIEVED IT.

© BRILLIANT ENTERPRISES 1977.

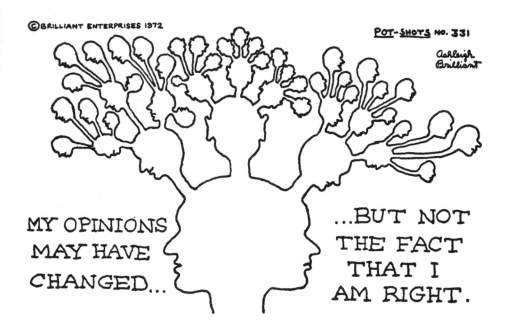

© BRILLIANT ENTERPRISES 1972

MY OPINIONS
MAY HAVE
CHANGED...

...BUT NOT
THE FACT
THAT I
AM RIGHT.

I ONLY OPENED

TO TELL YOU I'M CLOSED.

Ashleigh Brilliant

PLEASE RECONSIDER—
IT'S SO HARD
TO TAKE "GO TO HELL"
FOR AN ANSWER.

Ashleigh Brilliant

POT-SHOTS NO. 871

Ashleigh
Brilliant

HOW MUCH OF
YOUR INFLUENCE ON ME

IS A
RESULT OF
MY INFLUENCE
ON YOU?

You And Me
Person-To-Person Messages

The basic message situation is that of one mind speaking to another. But every mind is full of contradictory thoughts and feelings. The most effective brief cries therefore (as seen on the following pages), tend to be those which give voice to internal conflicts. It is the starkness of juxtaposed opposites that creates in the recipient mind a sense of "true-ness," combined with a feeling of "funny-ness" which softens the hard edges of the truth.

The usefulness of such messages often lies in their ability to ease the awkwardness of difficult situations. For example, many types of business (and other) negotiations begin with a certain wariness, and even hostility, between the two sides. The atmosphere can be considerably lightened if somebody has the courage to say, "I'll listen to your unreasonable demands if you'll consider my unacceptable offer."

A sense of having something in common, even if it's something silly, is perhaps the most healthy and beneficial of all human emotional states.

I like to think of you

On days that begin
With a morning.

©BRILLIANT ENTERPRISES 1974

If you notice
that I'm deceiving you,
I can't be deceiving you
very well.

Ashleigh Brilliant

If I didn't
understand you
so well,

I wouldn't
disagree
with you
so much.

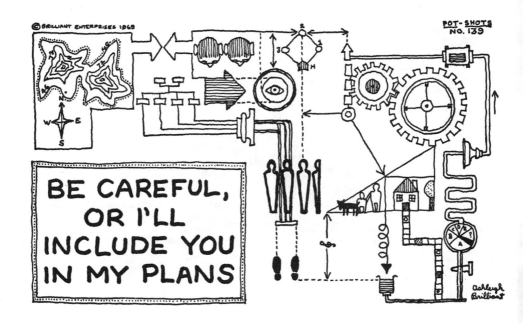

POT-SHOTS NO. 139

BE CAREFUL,
OR I'LL
INCLUDE YOU
IN MY PLANS

POT-SHOTS NO. 21 © BRILLIANT ENTERPRISES 1967

IF YOU DON'T LET ME
MAKE YOU HAPPY,
I'LL MAKE YOU SUFFER

Ashleigh
Brilliant

POT-SHOTS NO. 382

Ashleigh
Brilliant

IF ONLY
I KNEW
YOU LOVED ME,

I COULD FACE
THE UNCERTAINTY

OF WHETHER
I LOVE YOU.

WHY IS IT
TAKING SO LONG
FOR YOU TO
BRING OUT
ALL THE
GOOD IN ME?

Ashleigh Brilliant

YOU HAVE YOU
ON YOUR SIDE
BUT ALL I HAVE ON MY SIDE
IS ME

Ashleigh Brilliant

HOW MUCH
DO I LOVE YOU?

— LESS THAN
YOU'LL EVER KNOW.

Ashleigh Brilliant

IF ONLY
YOU WERE HERE
TO UPSET ME!

POT-SHOTS NO. 119

Ashleigh
Brilliant

WOULD YOU CARE
TO DRIFT AIMLESSLY

IN MY DIRECTION?

Ashleigh
Brilliant

POT-SHOTS NO. 88

WE OUGHT TO BE MORE CAREFUL —

OUR LOVE COULD DRAG ON
FOR YEARS AND YEARS

Ashleigh Brilliant
© BRILLIANT ENTERPRISES 1968

Please don't lie to me,
unless you're
absolutely sure
I'll never
find out the truth.

Ashleigh Brilliant

POT-SHOTS NO. 590.

Ashleigh
Brilliant

I CAN FORGIVE YOU FOR BEING WRONG,

BUT IT'S MUCH MUCH HARDER

TO FORGIVE YOU FOR BEING RIGHT.

50

How kind of you
to want to live
my life for me.

Ashleigh
Brilliant

**WHAT SHALL
I DO
UNTIL YOU
IMPROVE?**

Ashleigh Brilliant

Ashleigh
Brilliant

PLEASE DON'T
RECOMMEND ME
TO YOUR FRIENDS —

IT'S DIFFICULT ENOUGH
TO COPE WITH
YOU ALONE.

IF THINGS DON'T IMPROVE SOON I MAY HAVE TO ASK YOU TO STOP HELPING ME

Ashleigh Brilliant

FORGIVE ME NOW

tomorrow I may
no longer
feel guilty

Ashleigh Brilliant

REMEMBER ME?

I'M THE
ONE WHO
NEVER MADE
ANY IMPRESSION ON YOU.

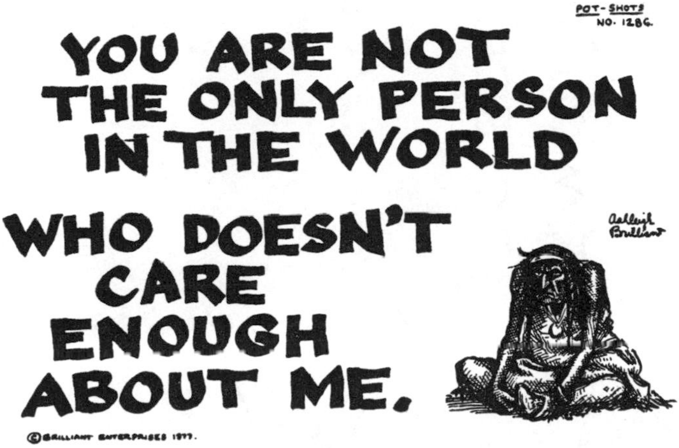

YOU ARE NOT THE ONLY PERSON IN THE WORLD

WHO DOESN'T CARE ENOUGH ABOUT ME.

WHY ARE YOU SO HARD TO IGNORE?

POT-SHOTS NO. 197.

IT WOULD BE NICE
TO SEE YOU AGAIN

AND AGAIN.

Ashleigh
Brilliant

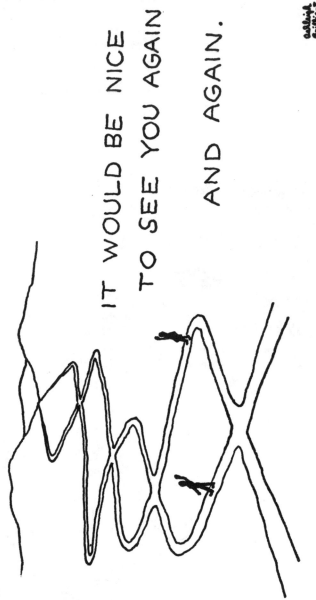

54

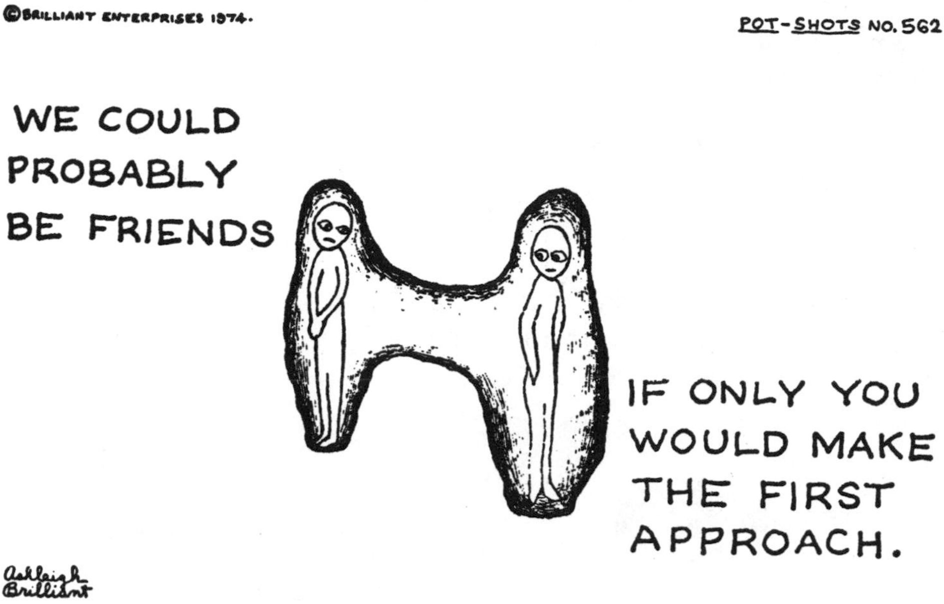

WE COULD
PROBABLY
BE FRIENDS

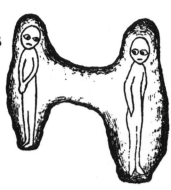

IF ONLY YOU
WOULD MAKE
THE FIRST
APPROACH.

Ashleigh Brilliant

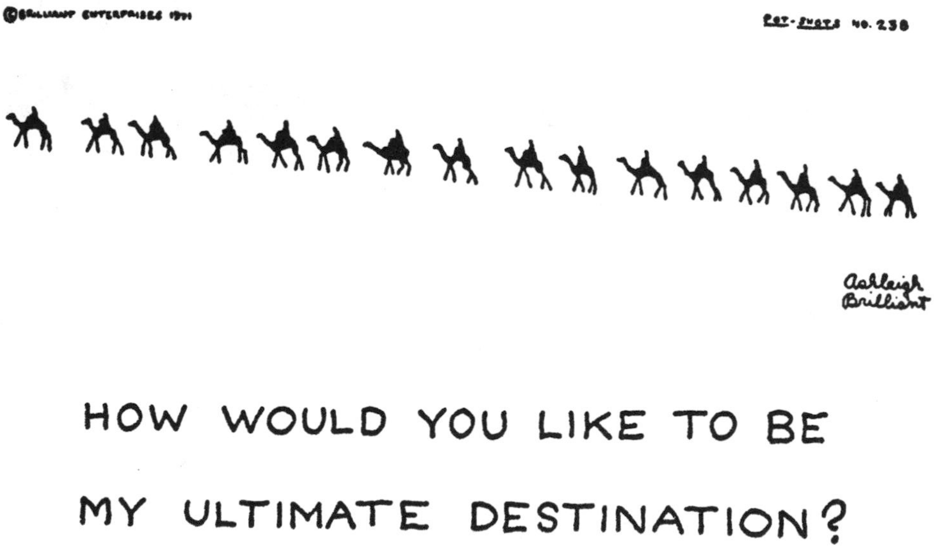

Ashleigh Brilliant

HOW WOULD YOU LIKE TO BE

MY ULTIMATE DESTINATION?

POT-SHOTS NO. 211

Isn't it a nice co-incidence

that you and I

are both alive at the same time!

© BRILLIANT ENTERPRISES 1974

POT-SHOTS NO. 508

I'M VERY SENSITIVE TO PLEASURE—

PLEASE DON'T COME TOO NEAR ME.

© BRILLIANT ENTERPRISES 1968

POT-SHOTS NO. 40

YOU CAN PLAY WITH MY LIFE

IF YOU'LL LET ME PLAY WITH YOURS

OUR LOVE IS GROWING

SO I
DON'T MIND

WATERING IT
OCCASIONALLY

WITH A FEW TEARS

*Ashleigh
Brilliant*

*Ashleigh
Brilliant*

DON'T EVER ASK ME

TO CHOOSE BETWEEN YOU AND HAPPINESS

BECAUSE I'D CHOOSE YOU EVERY TIME.

I DON'T
UNDERSTAND YOU

YOU DON'T
UNDERSTAND ME

WHAT ELSE
DO WE HAVE
IN COMMON?

POT SHOTS No. 208

57

WHY ISN'T THERE SOME CHEAP AND EASY WAY I CAN PROVE HOW MUCH YOU MEAN TO ME?

Ashleigh
Brilliant

© BRILLIANT ENTERPRISES 1977.

IF YOU CARED MORE FOR MY FEELINGS,

YOU WOULDN'T BE

SO SUCCESSFUL.

Ashleigh
Brilliant

© BRILLIANT ENTERPRISES 1974

© BRILLIANT ENTERPRISES 1969

PLEASE DON'T ASK ME WHAT THE SCORE IS —

I'M NOT EVEN SURE WHAT GAME WE'RE PLAYING.

Ashleigh
Brilliant

WHATEVER HAPPENED
TO ALL THE FUN
WE WERE GOING TO
HAVE TOGETHER?

LET'S STAY TOGETHER

AND DRAG
EACH OTHER
DOWN.

NOW THAT YOU
MENTION IT,

I DO
REMEMBER
LOVING YOU.

59

POT-SHOTS NO. 680

© BRILLIANT ENTERPRISES 1974

DON'T SHOOT!

WE MAY BOTH
BE ON THE
SAME SIDE.

Ashleigh Brilliant

The Strange World of Other People

Somewhere out there, beyond good old You and Me, are the Others, who sometimes call themselves Society. They refuse, on the one hand, to leave us completely alone; or, on the other, to be as concerned as we are about the really important things. Society has some very odd ideas about how we should behave, and at times appears to be controlled by a vast system of inter-connecting stupidities.

But it is also Society, bless it, who buys my postcards, and is thus at least gradually in the process of re-educating itself. I always take it as a pat on the back whenever (as often happens) I walk into some strange office in a strange city, and see the desk of some harassed worker decorated with one of my inspiring cards, perhaps the one which says, "If we all work together, we can totally disrupt the system."

I WISH ALL THE PEOPLE WHO SINCERELY WANT TO HELP ME COULD AGREE WITH EACH OTHER.

Ashleigh Brilliant

© BRILLIANT ENTERPRISES 1977.

PLEASE DON'T ASK ME

TO KEEP IN STEP —

IT'S HARD ENOUGH

Ashleigh Brilliant

JUST TO STAY IN LINE.

I GET ALONG
VERY WELL
WITH EVERYBODY,

EXCEPT ANIMALS
AND PEOPLE.

IN AN ORDERLY WORLD,

Ashleigh Brilliant

THERE'S
ALWAYS
A PLACE FOR
THE
DISORDERLY.

I'VE FOUND
THE SECRET
OF HAPPINESS —
TOTAL DISREGARD
OF EVERYBODY.

Ashleigh
Brilliant

POT-SHOTS NO. 363 ©BRILLIANT ENTERPRISES 1972

I WISH
I'D BEEN BORN WITH
AN UNFAIR ADVANTAGE,

INSTEAD OF HAVING TO
TRY TO ACQUIRE ONE.

Ashleigh Brilliant

©BRILLIANT ENTERPRISES 1974. POT-SHOTS NO. 614.

I HAD A TICKET
TO THE GOOD LIFE,

Ashleigh Brilliant

BUT SOMEHOW
COULD NEVER FIND
THE ENTRANCE.

I LIVE IN A WORLD OF MY OWN,

BUT VISITORS ARE ALWAYS WELCOME.

Ashleigh
Brilliant

WHAT I WANT IS ALL THE POWER AND NONE OF THE RESPONSIBILITY.

Ashleigh Brilliant

POT-SHOTS NO. 713

Ashleigh
Brilliant

OR MORE
CHANCE
TO
PARTICIPATE
IN IT.

I WANT
EITHER
LESS
CORRUPTION,

© BRILLIANT ENTERPRISES 1975.

66

POT-SHOTS NO. 784.

SHOULD I
ABIDE BY
THE RULES
UNTIL THEY'RE
CHANGED,

OR HELP SPEED THE CHANGE
BY BREAKING THEM?

© BRILLIANT ENTERPRISES 1975.

Ashleigh Brilliant

FOR GOD'S SAKE
TELL ME WHAT TO THINK!

Ashleigh
Brilliant

THE WORLD NEEDS
MORE PEOPLE LIKE US
AND FEWER LIKE THEM.

Ashleigh Brilliant

GOOD LEADERS
ARE SCARCE,

Ashleigh
Brilliant

SO I'M
FOLLOWING
MYSELF.

LET'S ORGANIZE THIS THING

Ashleigh Brilliant

AND TAKE ALL THE FUN OUT OF IT.

IT MAY OR MAY NOT BE WORTHWHILE, BUT IT STILL HAS TO BE DONE.

Ashleigh Brilliant

POT-SHOTS NO. 1328.

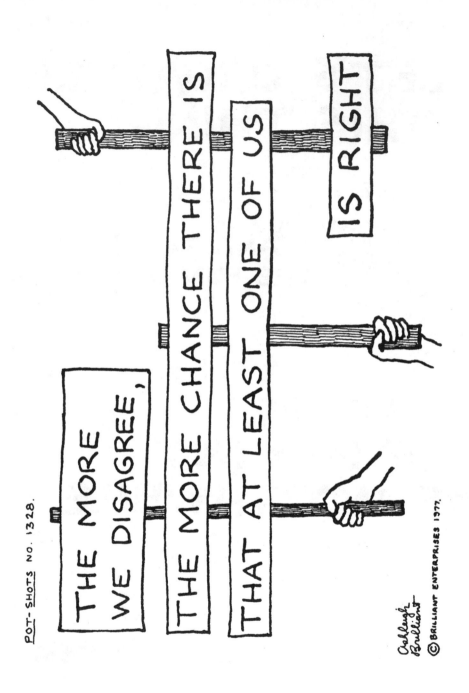

THE MORE
WE DISAGREE,
THE MORE CHANCE THERE IS
THAT AT LEAST ONE OF US
IS RIGHT

© BRILLIANT ENTERPRISES 1972

I DON'T CARE
WHAT THE WORLD
KNOWS
ABOUT ME

BUT I HOPE
MY MOTHER
NEVER
FINDS OUT.

Ashleigh Brilliant

© BRILLIANT ENTERPRISES 1971

I'M TOO BUSY
TO HAVE TIME FOR
ANYTHING
IMPORTANT.

Ashleigh Brilliant

POT-SHOTS NO. 1120.

NO MAN IS AN ISLAND

Ashleigh
Brilliant

BUT SOME OF US
ARE
LONG PENINSULAS.

POT-SHOTS NO. 949

IT'S INTERESTING
TO KNOW THAT
MANY DISTINGUISHED PEOPLE
HAVE BODIES
VERY SIMILAR
TO MINE.

Ashleigh
Brilliant

IF I DIDN'T HAVE MOST OF MY FRIENDS,

I WOULDN'T HAVE MOST OF MY PROBLEMS.

Ashleigh Brilliant

THANK YOU FOR NOT ANNOYING ME ANY MORE THAN YOU DO.

Ashleigh Brilliant

© BRILLIANT ENTERPRISES 1969

IT WAS ALL SO DIFFERENT BEFORE EVERYTHING CHANGED.

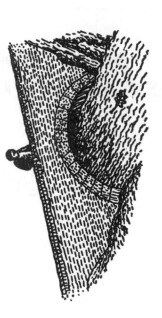

Ashleigh Brilliant

Time and Change

As we all know, change is definitely not what it used to be; but it is still rather mysterious and so, also, despite many improvements in clocks and watches, is the thing we call time. Of course, we all have a certain kind of inside information on these matters, and in many ways we know more than we think we do. We know, for example, how to travel into the future. What we don't know is how to go the other way, or how to go at any other speed than sixty minutes per hour.

But at least we are all in this together, and, as any writer of *Brilliant Thoughts* will tell you, the subject is one which everybody seems to respond to, even though the mood of the message may be quite a sad one. It's surprising how poignant a feeling can be conveyed in a very few words, when the subject is one on which both writer and reader are already well in tune. Actually, I never realized the true power of words until I began to limit my published utterances to seventeen of them.

The trouble is that words change like everything else, and sometimes come to mean exactly the opposite of what they once meant. ("Don't let me" meant "Don't hinder me" in Shakespeare's time.) I can only hope that they won't have changed too much more between the time of my transmission and your reception.

Everything
might be different
in the present,

if only one thing
had been different
in the past.

Ashleigh Brilliant

TODAY
IS
WHAT HAPPENED
TO YESTERDAY.

Ashleigh Brilliant

POT-SHOTS NO. 473

POT-SHOTS NO. 643

SOME PARTS OF THE PAST
MUST BE PRESERVED,

AND SOME OF
THE FUTURE
PREVENTED AT ALL COSTS.

POT-SHOTS NO. 1094.

MY GREAT AMBITION
IS
TO BUILD
SOMETHING
THAT WILL LAST,

AT LEAST UNTIL
I'VE FINISHED
BUILDING IT.

77

TOMORROW, THIS WILL BE PART OF THE UNCHANGEABLE PAST

BUT FORTUNATELY, IT CAN STILL BE CHANGED TODAY.

LOOK! BEFORE OUR VERY EYES,

THE FUTURE IS BECOMING THE PAST.

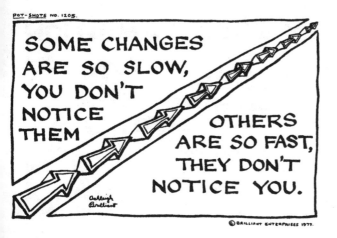

SOME CHANGES ARE SO SLOW, YOU DON'T NOTICE THEM

OTHERS ARE SO FAST, THEY DON'T NOTICE YOU.

POT-SHOTS NO. 1041.

BEFORE I KNEW
THE BEST PART
OF MY LIFE
HAD COME,

Ashleigh Brilliant

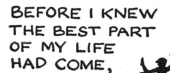

IT HAD GONE.

© BRILLIANT ENTERPRISES 1977.

© BRILLIANT ENTERPRISES 1976.   POT-SHOTS NO. 898.

*Time
will end
all my
troubles,*

*but I don't
always
approve of
Time's
methods.*

Ashleigh Brilliant

© BRILLIANT ENTERPRISES 1967   POT-SHOTS NO. 18

WHO WILL TAKE CARE OF THE WORLD
AFTER I'M GONE?

Ashleigh Brilliant

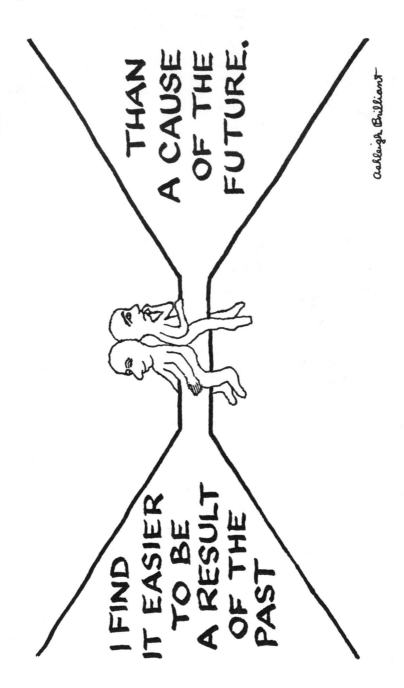

THAN
A CAUSE
OF THE
FUTURE.

I FIND
IT EASIER
TO BE
A RESULT
OF THE
PAST

Ashleigh Brilliant

Ashleigh Brilliant

I NEED MORE TIME

AND I PROBABLY ALWAYS WILL.

WHY DOES TROUBLE ALWAYS COME AT THE WRONG TIME?

Ashleigh Brilliant

Until recently,
I thought I was
someone I knew.

Ashleigh Brilliant

NOTHING IS
MORE QUIET
THAN THE SOUND
OF HAIR GOING GREY.

Ashleigh Brilliant

MY, HOW YOU'VE CHANGED

SINCE I'VE CHANGED.

Ashleigh Brilliant

PLEASE
DON'T
DISTURB
ME

WHILE
I'M
GROWING.

Ashleigh
Brilliant

WASTING TIME

Ashleigh
Brilliant

IS AN IMPORTANT PART
OF LIVING.

WHERE WILL IT ALL END?

— PROBABLY SOMEWHERE NEAR WHERE IT ALL BEGAN.

Ashleigh Brilliant

84

The World, and Other Illusions

Returning to what we call consciousness, we always ask first, "Where am I?" Everything that happens, happens somewhere. So it is only natural for some big thoughts on small postcards to be concerned with places real and unreal, and the problem of which is which. As you will see, I do occasionally think about the World (although the World is famous for refusing to think very much about me), and have even gone out now and then to look at it, sometimes by hitch-hiking. I discovered that you could always get rides more easily if you carried a sign showing your destination. Now my cards like those in this chapter, serve a similar function, helping people to realize that we are all going the same way.

SOMEHOW IT SEEMS
THE WORLD IS HAVING
MORE EFFECT
ON ME

THAN I'M HAVING ON THE WORLD.

Ashleigh Brilliant

*Ashleigh
Brilliant*

I FEEL
DISILLUSIONED ~

DO YOU
HAVE ANY
GOOD NEW
ILLUSIONS?

I HAVE ABANDONED MY SEARCH FOR TRUTH,

AND AM NOW LOOKING

FOR A GOOD FANTASY.

Ashleigh Brilliant

EITHER THIS
LIFE I'M IN
IS VERY DREAM-LIKE,

OR THIS
DREAM I'M IN
IS VERY LIFE-LIKE.

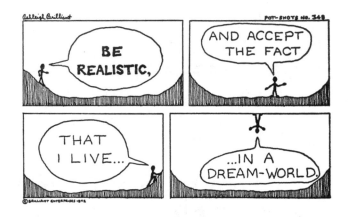

Ashleigh Brilliant

BE
REALISTIC,

AND ACCEPT
THE FACT

THAT
I LIVE...

...IN A
DREAM-WORLD.

WHERE DO I GO,

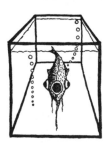

NOW THAT I'VE
REACHED
MY LIMITS?

IT'S REALLY
QUITE A SIMPLE CHOICE:

LIFE, DEATH,
OR LOS ANGELES.

POT-SHOTS
NO. 79

© BRILLIANT ENTERPRISES 1968

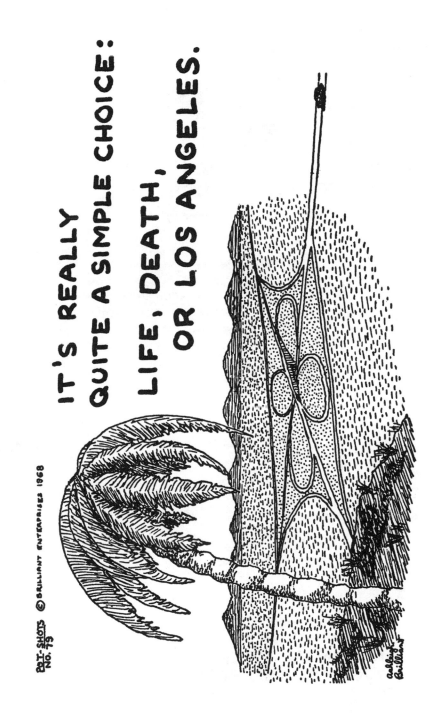

I LIKE TO TRAVEL —

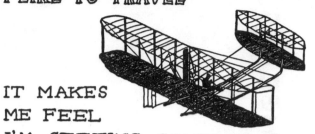

IT MAKES
ME FEEL
I'M GETTING SOMEWHERE.

© Brilliant Enterprises 1971

Ashleigh Brilliant

© Brilliant Enterprises 1971

POT-SHOTS NO. 278

DUE TO CIRCUMSTANCES
BEYOND MY CONTROL,
I AM MASTER OF MY FATE
AND CAPTAIN OF MY SOUL.

Ashleigh Brilliant

© Brilliant Enterprises 1975.

POT-SHOTS NO. 830

Ashleigh
Brilliant

LIVING ON EARTH
MAY BE EXPENSIVE,

BUT IT INCLUDES
AN ANNUAL FREE TRIP
AROUND THE SUN.

I DON'T GREATLY NEED THE OUTSIDE WORLD,

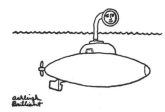

but I do
like to know
that it's
still there.

aahleigh
Brilliant

ARE YOU
ON MY SIDE...

OR THE
WORLD'S
SIDE?

aahleigh
Brilliant

PLEASE HELP KEEP THE WORLD CLEAN: OTHERS MAY WISH TO USE IT.

aahleigh
Brilliant

91

IT'LL BE A
NICE WORLD
IF THEY EVER
GET IT FINISHED

KEEP UP THE GOOD WORK!

**BUT PLEASE
DON'T ASK
ME TO HELP.**

ALL THE EVIDENCE CONCERNING THE UNIVERSE HAS NOT YET BEEN COLLECTED,

SO THERE'S STILL HOPE.

Ashleigh Brilliant

ACCORDING TO ALL THE LATEST REPORTS,

Ashleigh Brilliant

THERE WAS NO TRUTH IN ANY OF THE EARLIER REPORTS.

THERE'S ONLY ONE EVERYTHING.

Ashleigh Brilliant

EVERYTHING IS CONTROLLED BY A SMALL EVIL GROUP

TO WHICH, UNFORTUNATELY, NOBODY I KNOW BELONGS.

Ashleigh Brilliant

GETTING THERE IS ONLY HALF AS FAR

AS GETTING THERE AND BACK.

Ashleigh Brilliant

POT-SHOTS NO. 1172

I'LL NEVER SEE
ALL THE PLACES,
OR READ
ALL THE BOOKS,

BUT
FORTUNATELY,

THEY'RE NOT ALL RECOMMENDED.

Ashleigh Brilliant

POT-SHOTS NO. 588

Every time
I close the door on Reality,
it comes in
through the window.

Ashleigh Brilliant

 POT-SHOTS NO. 388

IF YOU
LIKED
THE
EARTH

YOU'LL
LOVE
HEAVEN

Ashleigh Brilliant

IS THERE A LIFE
BEFORE BREAKFAST ?

*Ashleigh
Brilliant*

I'M LOOKING FOR
THE PERFECT PILLOW —

I THINK IT'S
SOMEWHERE
NEAR YOURS.

*Ashleigh
Brilliant*

What Is Your Pleasure?

Strange as it seems, life can actually be enjoyable; and there are even some people who believe that the good parts are worth the bad parts. Be that as it may, no survey of the universe would be complete without at least some reference to the odd phenomenon of human pleasure. No doubt it will not be too much longer before medical science, which has done us so many other services, will enable us to stimulate directly and at will the pleasure-centers of the brain, thereby rendering completely obsolete all the old-fashioned pleasure-devices, contrivances, practices, and substances, all the things we had to do with and to our bodies in order to get fleeting feelings of enjoyment. Until that happy day, we must painfully extract whatever entertainment is available from food, sex, games, spectacles, and various other titillations, trying somehow to prove that pleasure can be fun.

ALL I ASK IS
A CHANCE TO PROVE THAT

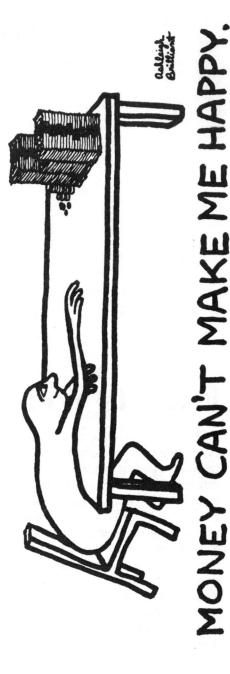

MONEY CAN'T MAKE ME HAPPY.

ONE OF MY FAVORITE WAYS TO END A GAME IS BY WINNING.

Ashleigh Brilliant

IF YOU CAN'T LEARN TO DO IT WELL,

Ashleigh Brilliant

LEARN TO ENJOY DOING IT BADLY.

THE KIND OF DANGER I MOST ENJOY

IS THE KIND I CAN WATCH FROM A SAFE PLACE.

MY OBJECT IS TO SAVE THE WORLD,

WHILE STILL LEADING A PLEASANT LIFE.

THE SUREST WAY
TO REMAIN A WINNER
IS TO WIN ONCE,
AND THEN NOT PLAY ANY MORE.

© BRILLIANT ENTERPRISES 1974.

© BRILLIANT ENTERPRISES 1977   POT-SHOTS
NO. 1268.

I WILL STOP
AT NOTHING
TO REACH MY
OBJECTIVE,

BUT ONLY BECAUSE
MY BRAKES
ARE DEFECTIVE.

Ashleigh Brilliant

© BRILLIANT ENTERPRISES 1968

WHEN ALL ELSE FAILS,
EAT!

POT-SHOTS NO. 142

101

ANYTHING IS GOOD IF IT'S MADE OF CHOCOLATE

I DON'T NEED
A GREAT DEAL OF LOVE
BUT I DO NEED
A STEADY SUPPLY.

But after you have gone

I will still have

PEANUT BUTTER!

Ashleigh
Brilliant

HELP IMPROVE MY APPEARANCE —

I'M MUCH
BETTER-LOOKING
WHEN I'VE BEEN
HUGGED.

WHAT WOULD LIFE BE

WITHOUT ME?

Ashleigh
Brilliant

ENJOY YOURSELF

WHILE YOU'RE
STILL OLD.

Ashleigh
Brilliant

THERE HAS BEEN
AN ALARMING INCREASE

IN THE NUMBER
OF THINGS

I KNOW
NOTHING ABOUT.

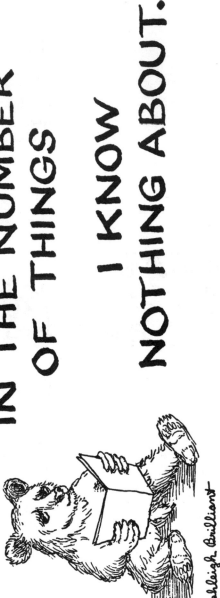

Ashleigh Brilliant

A Thousand Thinks

Brilliant Thoughts, as a whole, express no particular philosophy or point of view, and are no more intended to than a window is meant to express an opinion about what you see through it. But each separate *Thought* does have something very definite to say, particularly those in this section, which are largely concerned with religion, philosophy, morality, and knowledge. Although it has been traditionally felt that such matters do not readily lend themselves to popular treatment, my experience indicates that the public is willing to give its total attention to any subject, no matter how profound, so long as you present it with wit, intelligence, and compassion, and discuss it fully from all sides in no more than seventeen words.

Ministers of various persuasions often write to tell me that they have used my *Thoughts* as texts for sermons. This conjures up pleasant fantasies about my works somehow becoming a new kind of Bible. Every great movement needs a Holy Book of some kind—could there be a "holy postcard"?

I NEVER GO ANYWHERE

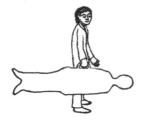

WITHOUT
MY
SOUL.

Ashleigh Brilliant

I MAY BE INFINITELY SMALLER THAN SOME THINGS,

BUT I'M INFINITELY LARGER THAN OTHERS

Ashleigh Brilliant

THERE'S NOTHING
VERY MYSTERIOUS
ABOUT ME,

EXCEPT THAT
NOBODY REALLY KNOWS

MY ORIGIN, PURPOSE, OR DESTINATION.

Ashleigh Brilliant

What makes the Universe so hard to comprehend

is that there's nothing to compare it with.

Ashleigh Brilliant

I don't have any solution, but I certainly admire the problem.

Ashleigh Brilliant

POT-SHOTS NO. 1347.

Ashleigh
Brilliant

LIFE
MAY
HAVE
NO
MEANING

OR,
EVEN
WORSE,

IT MAY
HAVE
A MEANING
OF WHICH
I DISAPPROVE.

POT-SHOTS NO.930

Ashleigh Brilliant

I HAVE A THEORY THAT IT'S IMPOSSIBLE TO PROVE ANYTHING, BUT I CAN'T PROVE IT.

© BRILLIANT ENTERPRISES 1976

POT-SHOTS NO. 717

Ashleigh Brilliant

SCIENCE MAY SOMEDAY DISCOVER WHAT FAITH HAS ALWAYS KNOWN.

© BRILLIANT ENTERPRISES 1975.

It's possible that my whole purpose in life is simply to serve as a warning to others.

Ashleigh Brilliant

Ashleigh Brilliant

SURELY
I DESERVE
SOME KIND OF
RECOGNITION

FOR ALL THE
BAD THINGS
I HAVEN'T DONE.

THIS LIFE IS MINE

Ashleigh Brilliant

SOME OF IT
WAS GIVEN TO ME;

THE REST, I MADE MYSELF.

I'M JUST
MOVING CLOUDS
TODAY—

TOMORROW
I'LL TRY
MOUNTAINS.

Ashleigh Brilliant

IF ONLY I HAD FEWER NEEDS,

AND YOU HAD MORE ABILITY

TO SATISFY THEM!

Ashleigh
Brilliant

I am currently
going through
a difficult transition period
called "Life."

Ashleigh
Brilliant

OF COURSE I HAVE A PURPOSE --
TO FIND A PURPOSE.

Ashleigh
Brilliant

BRING ME A DICTIONARY:

I WANT
TO KNOW
THE MEANING
OF LIFE.

Ashleigh Brilliant

EDUCATION

HAS SO MUCH TO LEARN!

Ashleigh
Brilliant

SCHOOL IS BAD ENOUGH—
BUT AT LEAST
I'M NOT LETTING THEM
TEACH ME ANYTHING.

IF YOU LEARN ONE USELESS THING EVERY DAY, IN A SINGLE YEAR YOU'LL LEARN 365 USELESS THINGS.

Ashleigh Brilliant

YOUR REASONING
IS EXCELLENT —

*Ashleigh
Brilliant*

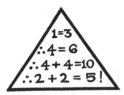

$$1 = 3$$
$$\therefore 4 = 6$$
$$\therefore 4 + 4 = 10$$
$$\therefore 2 + 2 = 5 !$$

**IT'S ONLY
YOUR BASIC
ASSUMPTIONS
THAT ARE WRONG.**

WHATEVER
BECAME OF
ETERNAL
TRUTH ?

*Ashleigh
Brilliant*

HOW TIRED I FEEL!

**I UNDERSTOOD
SO MUCH
TODAY.**

*Ashleigh
Brilliant*

**FUNDAMENTALLY,
THERE MAY BE
NO BASIS
FOR
ANYTHING.**

*Ashleigh
Brilliant*

*Ashleigh
Brilliant*

THINKING ABOUT IT
IS EASIER THAN DOING IT —

BUT SO FAR,
I HAVEN'T EVEN
THOUGHT ABOUT IT.

**IT OCCURRED TO ME LATELY
THAT NOTHING HAS
OCCURRED TO ME LATELY.**

Ashleigh Brilliant

Ashleigh
Brilliant

IF LIFE IS MERELY A JOKE,

THE QUESTION STILL REMAINS:

FOR WHOSE AMUSEMENT?

HISTORY IS ON OUR SIDE

Ashleigh
Brilliant

as long as
we can
control
the historians.

LIFE CAN BE SO TRAGIC —

YOU'RE HERE TODAY

AND HERE TOMORROW

Ashleigh Brilliant © BRILLIANT ENTERPRISES 1967

Life and Other Problems

Let us be honest with ourselves: life is something which is here to stay—at least, as long as *we* are. It involves us totally—days, nights, and sometimes even weekends. It is no respecter of age or gender or social position, and even animals are said to have it.

What to do about it? Modern research suggests that it is all in the mind, and can be kept entirely under control with an occasional shock treatment. Rising to this occasion, I have devised many of the *Brilliant Thoughts* in this section to administer the necessary psychic jolts. Call it, if you will, in the great tradition of the "dirty postcard," a kind of philosophical pornography. Unfortunately, my statements are not always given credit for being as outrageous as they truly are. Upton Sinclair said of his novel *The Jungle* that he aimed at the public's heart and hit its stomach. Sometimes I feel I have aimed at the public's brain, and merely hit its funny-bone.

119

I'M SECRETLY
VERY INTERESTED
IN LIFE.

POT-SHOTS NO. 103

Ashleigh
Brilliant

POT-SHOTS NO. 420

MY PICTURE
OF THE WORLD
KEEPS CHANGING
BEFORE I CAN
GET IT INTO FOCUS.

Ashleigh
Brilliant

120

IF YOU'RE CAREFUL ENOUGH, NOTHING BAD OR GOOD WILL EVER HAPPEN TO YOU.

Ashleigh
Brilliant

CHEER UP!

THINGS MAY BE GETTING WORSE AT A SLOWER RATE.

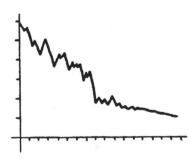

Ashleigh Brilliant

MAYBE I'M LUCKY
TO BE GOING
SO SLOWLY

BECAUSE
I MAY BE GOING
IN THE WRONG DIRECTION

BY DOING
JUST A LITTLE
EVERY DAY,

*Ashleigh
Brilliant*

I CAN
GRADUALLY
LET THE TASK
COMPLETELY
OVERWHELM ME.

© BRILLIANT ENTERPRISES 1977.

*Ashleigh
Brilliant*

IF I DON'T DO
THE THINGS
THAT ARE NOT
WORTH DOING,
WHO WILL?

© BRILLIANT ENTERPRISES 1974

© BRILLIANT ENTERPRISES 1968   POT-SHOTS NO. 66

NOTHING
REALLY MATTERS

EXCEPT A
FEW THINGS

THAT REALLY
DON'T MATTER
VERY MUCH

Ashleigh
Brilliant

POT-SHOTS NO. 485

I MEANT
NO HARM BY
STAYING ALIVE!
I ONLY DID IT
FOR A JOKE!

© BRILLIANT ENTERPRISES 1974

Ashleigh
Brilliant

© BRILLIANT ENTERPRISES 1870   POT-SHOTS NO. 151

NO USE GETTING
TOO INVOLVED IN LIFE
— I'M ONLY HERE FOR
A LIMITED TIME.

Ashleigh
Brilliant

I THINK I'LL JUST SIT HERE

AND WAIT TILL LIFE GETS EASIER

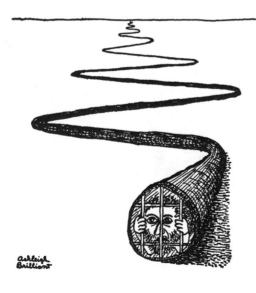

OH WELL,
I GUESS THIS IS JUST
GOING TO BE
ONE OF THOSE LIFETIMES!

NO, LIFE ISN'T WHAT I WANTED --

HAVEN'T YOU GOT ANYTHING ELSE?

I AM FIGHTING FOR SURVIVAL

in my own
sweet and
gentle way.

Ashleigh Brilliant

SOMETIMES I GET
AN ALMOST IRRESISTIBLE URGE
TO GO ON LIVING

Ashleigh Brilliant

I'M TRYING TO LIVE MY LIFE —

A TASK SO DIFFICULT,
IT HAS NEVER BEEN
ATTEMPTED BEFORE.

SOMEDAY I'LL GET MY BIG CHANCE—

OR HAVE I ALREADY HAD IT?

Ashleigh Brilliant

ALL I WANT IS

A LITTLE MORE

THAN I'LL

EVER GET.

Ashleigh Brilliant

I FEEL MUCH BETTER,
NOW THAT I'VE
GIVEN UP HOPE.

Ashleigh
Brilliant

Ashleigh Brilliant

ONE POSSIBLE REASON
WHY THINGS
AREN'T GOING
ACCORDING
TO PLAN

IS THAT
THERE NEVER
WAS A PLAN.

I HOPE
THE LIFE-INSPECTOR
DOESN'T
COME AROUND
WHILE
I HAVE
MY LIFE
IN SUCH A MESS.

Ashleigh Brilliant

I HOPE I GET WHAT I WANT

Ashleigh
Brilliant

Before
I stop
wanting it.

I'M DOING MY PART TO HELP PRESERVE LIFE ON EARTH

Ashleigh
Brilliant

BY TRYING TO PRESERVE MY OWN.

I RECENTLY
HAD MY PROBLEMS
ON THE RUN,

Ashleigh
Brilliant

BUT NOW
THEY'VE
RE-GROUPED,
AND ARE
MAKING
ANOTHER
ATTACK.

It takes
a special kind
of courage

to face
what we all have to face.

Ashleigh
Brilliant

Ashleigh
Brilliant

TO BE SURE
OF HITTING
THE TARGET,

SHOOT FIRST

AND, WHATEVER YOU HIT,
CALL IT THE TARGET.

POT-SHOTS NO. 1374.

I'M GROWING OUT OF
SOME OF MY PROBLEMS,

BUT
THERE ARE OTHERS
I'M GROWING INTO.

POT-SHOTS NO. 1044.

BY TRYING
VERY HARD
TO
IMPROVE
THINGS,

I AM
OFTEN ABLE
TO MAKE THEM
MUCH WORSE.

POT-SHOTS NO. 312.

IF YOU DON'T DO IT,
YOU'LL NEVER KNOW
WHAT WOULD HAVE HAPPENED
IF YOU HAD DONE IT.

133

POT-SHOTS NO. 1146

I wish
I had done
some of the
hard things

when they were
easier to do.

Ashleigh
Brilliant

POT-SHOTS NO. 918.

Ashleigh
Brilliant

HOW CAN I
POSSIBLY
HAVE COME
SO FAR,

AND YET
STILL HAVE
SO FAR TO GO?

Ashleigh
Brilliant

EVERY SUCCESSFUL PERSON HAS HAD FAILURES

BUT
REPEATED FAILURE
IS NO GUARANTEE
OF
EVENTUAL SUCCESS.

© BRILLIANT ENTERPRISES 1977.

POT-SHOTS NO. 472

MY LIFE

WOULD
BE
VERY
EMPTY

Ashleigh
Brilliant

IF I HAD
NOTHING
TO REGRET.

© BRILLIANT ENTERPRISES 1974

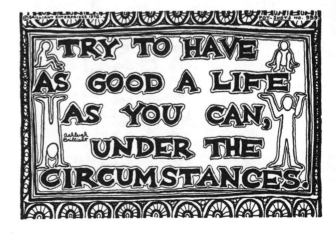

TRY TO HAVE AS GOOD A LIFE AS YOU CAN, UNDER THE CIRCUMSTANCES.

© BRILLIANT ENTERPRISES 1974

PLEASE
DON'T
TELL ME
TO RELAX—

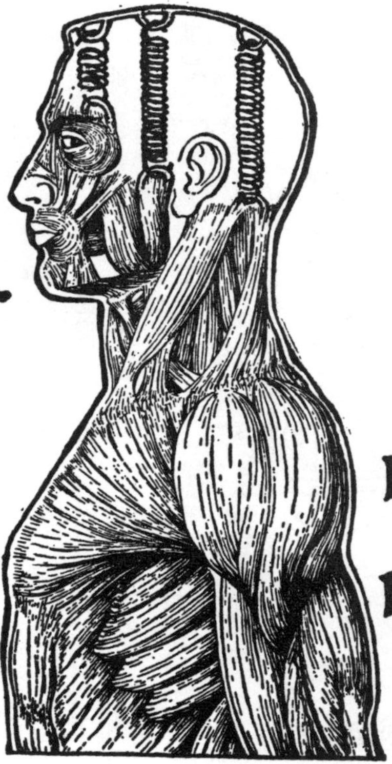

IT'S ONLY
MY TENSION
THAT'S
HOLDING ME
TOGETHER.

Ashleigh
Brilliant

136

Health, Death, and Other Mysterious Conditions

Who or what is healthy? It's getting harder and harder to tell. And the latest uncertainty being inflicted on us by Science is that we are no longer sure when we are dead. It used to be that the only forms of literature which discussed these matters were heavy books and even heavier tombstones. My postcards provide a lighter forum. Nowadays people actually write to ask if they may quote a *Brilliant Thought* on their own tombstone. I grant permission, on condition that they also include on the stone a correct copyright notice. (Thus one of my fantasies has been fulfilled—to write words so meaningful that people would want to carve them in stone. Another fantasy has been to become required reading in schools and colleges. This too has been fulfilled, in the form of many requests to be quoted and reproduced in text-books.)

One group to whom these particular messages seem to have special appeal are those who call themselves "Immortalists"—people who believe that what we call "death" may be only some kind of disease for which we haven't yet developed a cure. I sincerely wish them and their movement good health and long life.

I WISH
I HAD
MORE
ENERGY...

...OR
LESS
AMBITION.

Ashleigh
Brilliant

FORCE YOURSELF
TO RELAX

Ashleigh
Brilliant

Ashleigh
Brilliant

IT'S
VERY
INCONVENIENT
TO BE
MORTAL ~

YOU
NEVER KNOW
WHEN
EVERYTHING
MAY SUDDENLY
STOP HAPPENING.

©BRILLIANT ENTERPRISES 1976.

©BRILLIANT ENTERPRISES 1974.

POT-SHOTS NO. 698

Ashleigh
Brilliant

IS DEATH
LEGALLY
BINDING?

WHAT SHOULD I DO IF MY PROBLEMS AREN'T ALL SOLVED BY THE TIME I DIE?

TELL THE SCIENTISTS TO HURRY——

I DON'T WANT TO DIE BEFORE THEY DISCOVER HOW TO SAVE ME.

I AM NOT DEAD YET

but watch for further reports.

**I could live
a better life,
if I had
a better mind
and a better body.**

Ashleigh
Brilliant

Ashleigh
Brilliant

I'M DOING
WHAT I CAN
TO
PROLONG
MY LIFE,
HOPING THAT
SOMEDAY
I'LL LEARN
WHAT IT'S FOR.

WHAT CAUSES
THE MYSTERIOUS DEATH
OF
EVERYBODY?

Ashleigh
Brilliant

©BRILLIANT ENTERPRISES 1977.

Ashleigh
Brilliant

I may be gone tomorrow,

but that won't mean

that I wasn't here today.

©BRILLIANT ENTERPRISES 1976.

©BRILLIANT ENTERPRISES 1977

POT-SHOTS NO. 1124.

I WANT
ALL MY
POSTHUMOUS MEDALS
IN ADVANCE.

Ashleigh Brilliant

I NEED A GOOD
IMAGINARY CURE
FOR MY PAINFUL
IMAGINARY AILMENT.

Ashleigh Brilliant

Ashleigh Brilliant

HALF THE TIME
I'M TOO COLD,
AND HALF
TOO HOT ~

SO, AT LEAST
ON AVERAGE,
I'M COMFORTABLE.

ONE THING ABOUT PAIN:

Ashleigh Brilliant

IT PROVES

YOU'RE

ALIVE!

143

MY ARMS ARE ACHING TO HOLD YOU

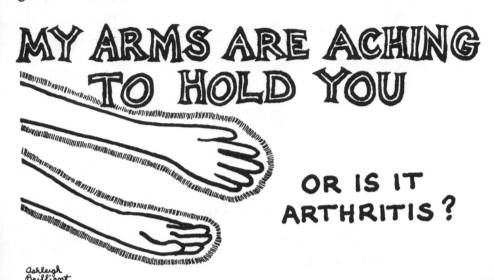

OR IS IT ARTHRITIS?

Ashleigh Brilliant

SOMETIMES THE BEST MEDICINE IS TO STOP TAKING SOMETHING.

Ashleigh Brilliant

AT THE END
OF MY LIFE,
THERE'LL BE A GOOD REST,

AND NO FURTHER
ACTIVITIES
ARE SCHEDULED.

Ashleigh Brilliant

I HOPE
THE DAY AFTER I DIE
IS A NICE DAY.

Ashleigh Brilliant

Ashleigh Brilliant

IF I CAN
SURVIVE DEATH,
I CAN PROBABLY
SURVIVE
ANYTHING.

145

YES, BUT
WHICH SELF
DO YOU WANT
ME TO BE?

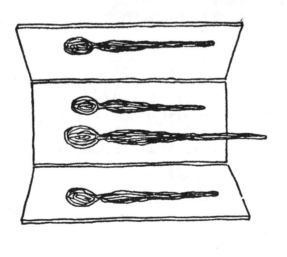

Ashleigh
Brilliant

The Crowded Self

When my own strange thoughts began to be widely circulated as postcards, it pleased and surprised me to learn that many counsellors, psychiatrists, and others working in the field of Mental Health were finding them useful in their work, particularly (it seems) for stimulating their patients to think and talk about their own problems. This had never been any part of my original purpose—in fact, I was astonished. What had I done to become suddenly so useful to so many people? Nothing that many or most others couldn't do if they had thought of it. I had simply put many small pieces of myself on many small pieces of paper, and let them loose. They were about *my* problems, not yours. Suppose more people advertised their thoughts and feelings in this way! (Or in other ways!) Perhaps there wouldn't be so many mental health problems. (Or would there be *more*?)

One of the biggest of these problems apparently revolves around the question, "Who or what am I (or is me)?"

For some reason, this is a question rarely asked or discussed in the popular media. Yet our whole concept of "self" is currently undergoing drastic revision. We are no longer so sure as we once were that an "individual" is really in-dividual, that is, incapable of being divided. Blood transfusions, organ transplants, artificial body parts—and eventually, no doubt, the divided, transplanted, and re-arranged brain: perhaps these are all merely stages on the journey to a new Extended Self. In the hope that this may be so, I encourage you to consider that the self in the following messages may, at least occasionally, be yours.

THE PART OF THE WORLD
WHICH I FIND
MOST PUZZLING

IS THE PART
CALLED
"ME"

Ashleigh Brilliant

Ashleigh Brilliant

I'M LEARNING
ABOUT PEOPLE
THE HARD WAY—

BY
BEING
ONE.

THE ODDS ARE
A MILLION
TO ONE

Ashleigh
Brilliant

AGAINST MY BEING
ONE IN A MILLION.

© BRILLIANT ENTERPRISES 1973

© BRILLIANT ENTERPRISES 1977.

MY TRUE VALUE

DEPENDS ENTIRELY
ON
WHAT YOU
COMPARE
ME WITH.

Ashleigh
Brilliant

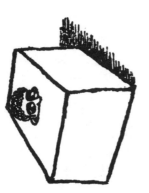

CONFIDENTIALLY,

I HAVE NOTHING
WORTH HIDING.

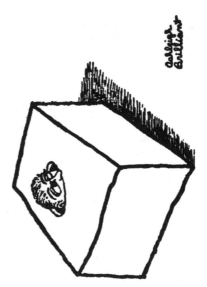

Ashleigh Brilliant

I AM
UNCONDITIONALLY
GUARANTEED
TO BE
FULL OF DEFECTS.

Ashleigh Brilliant

IF YOU HAVE
DOUBTS ABOUT ME,
DON'T WORRY—

I HAVE MANY
ABOUT MYSELF.

Ashleigh Brilliant

SOME
PARTS OF ME
ARE SO PRIVATE
THAT I MYSELF
HAVE
NO
KNOWLEDGE OF THEM.

Ashleigh Brilliant

© BRILLIANT ENTERPRISES 1976

WHEN YOU'RE BORN, YOU'RE TAKING A BIG CHANCE.

Ashleigh
Brilliant

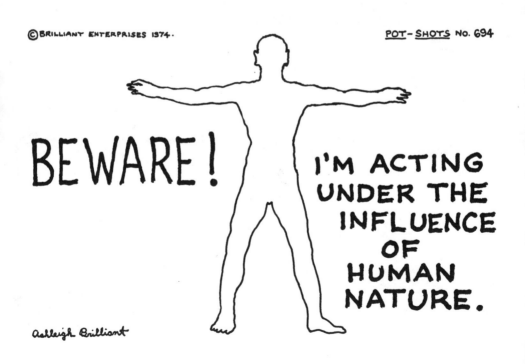

BEWARE !

I'M ACTING UNDER THE INFLUENCE OF HUMAN NATURE.

Ashleigh Brilliant

I'M READY TO GIVE UP THE STRUGGLE,

BUT CAN'T FIND ANYBODY TO SURRENDER TO.

Ashleigh Brilliant

IF YOU WANT TO PUT YOURSELF ON THE MAP,

PUBLISH YOUR OWN MAP.

Ashleigh Brilliant

SINGLE-HANDEDLY, I HAVE FOUGHT MY WAY INTO THIS HOPELESS MESS.

Ashleigh
Brilliant

MOST OF MY FAULTS

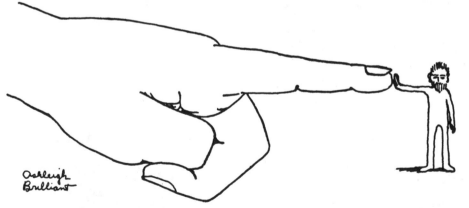

Ashleigh
Brilliant

ARE NOT MY FAULT.

POT-SHOTS NO. 648

I WISH THEY'D PASS MORE LAWS

TO PROTECT ME FROM MYSELF.

Ashleigh Brilliant

 POT-SHOTS NO. 36

HELP!
I'M TRAPPED IN
A HUMAN BODY!

Ashleigh Brilliant

 POT-SHOTS NO. 293

I'M IN SEARCH
OF MYSELF —

HAVE YOU SEEN ME ANYWHERE?

Ashleigh Brilliant

IF I DON'T HAVE SOME INSANITY SOON, I'LL GO MAD!

Ashleigh Brilliant

If I go out of my mind,

I'll do it quietly, so as not to disturb you.

Ashleigh Brilliant

DESPITE ALL APPEARANCES, I AM A THINKING, FEELING, HUMAN BEING.

Ashleigh Brilliant

Ashleigh Brilliant

I HAD
SOME HAPPINESS
ONCE,

BUT WE
MOVED AWAY,

AND I HAD TO
LEAVE IT BEHIND.

If only
I could be
respected

Without having to be
respectable!

Ashleigh Brilliant

I WROTE MYSELF A THREATENING LETTER

AND RECEIVED A DEFIANT REPLY.

ONE OF THE WORST OF MY MANY FAULTS

IS THAT I'M TOO CRITICAL OF MYSELF.

New members
are urgently needed
in the
Society for Prevention
of Cruelty to Yourself.

POT-SHOTS NO. 546
Ashleigh
Brilliant

I WORK VERY HARD

PLEASE DON'T EXPECT ME
TO THINK AS WELL.

POT-SHOTS NO. 517
Ashleigh
Brilliant

PLEASE DON'T SUPPLY ANY MORE INFORMATION

I'm already
Too well informed.

POT-SHOTS NO. 575
Ashleigh
Brilliant

IF I HAD
BETTER TOOLS,

I COULD
MORE EFFECTIVELY
DEMONSTRATE

MY TOTAL
INCOMPETENCE.

159

I'M WORKING UNDER A SLIGHT HANDICAP.

I HAPPEN TO BE HUMAN.

Ashleigh Brilliant

160